Date Due

Documenting World War II

War in the Pacific

Sean Sheehan

New York

Published in 2009 by The Rosen Publishing Group Inc.
29 East 21st Street, New York, NY 10010

Copyright © 2009 Wayland/The Rosen Publishing Group, Inc.

First Edition

Editor: Camilla Lloyd
Consultants: Dr. R. Gerald Hughes and Dr. James Vaughan
Designer: Phipps Design
Maps: Ian Thompson
Picture researcher: Diana Morris
Indexer and proofreader: Patience Coster

Picture Acknowledgments: The author and publisher would like to thank the
following for allowing their pictures to be reproduced in this publication: Cover
photographs: BL: Corbis, BR: Cody Image; AKG Images: 1, 25, 26, 44; Australian
War Memorial: negative number 135867: 8; Barnaby's Studios/Mary Evans Picture
Library: 4; Cody Images: 6, 15, 22, 24, 31, 33, 34, 36, 38, 41, 42; Corbis: 1, 11;
Columbia Pictures/Album/AKG Image: 16; Hulton-Deutsch Collection/Corbis: 28;
Keystone Images/Getty Images: 14; Minnesota Historical Society/Corbis: 19;
Rykoff Collection/Corbis: 23; Time & Life Pictures/Getty Images: 13, 17.

Every attempt has been made to clear copyright. Should there be any inadvertent
omission please apply to the publisher for rectification.

Library of Congress Cataloging-in-Publication Data

Sheehan, Sean, 1951-
  War in the Pacific / Sean Sheehan. -- 1st ed.
     p. cm. -- (Documenting World War II)
  Includes bibliographical references and index.
  ISBN 978-1-4042-1859-8 (lib. bndg.)
  1. World War, 1939-1945--Campaigns--Pacific Area. I. Title.
  D767.S5295 2008
  940.54'26--dc22
                                          2007041761

Manufactured in China

CONTENTS

Background to war

World War II (WWII) started in 1939 when Britain and France declared war on Germany as a result of the German invasion of Poland. The causes of the Pacific War, which became part of WWII, were not directly related to the events in Europe. The background to the Pacific War lay with rivalry between the United States (U.S.) and Japan. Both countries, in their different ways, believed in their right to influence what happened in the Pacific region. They were also alike in the fact that

The most modern coal mine in Kailan in north China (output of five million tons of coal per year) was occupied by the Japanese in 1937 as a result of the fighting in Manchuria.

they both looked to military power as a means of establishing their influence in the region.

China was an undeveloped country without a single government for its vast territory. Japan and the U.S. were in opposition over who would be able to assert control over this country. Japan and the U.S. both wanted to invest in China and potentially gain from the profits of these investments.

Japan began its campaign by occupying Manchuria, a region northeast of China, in 1931. Six years later, this led to war with China, when in 1937, Japan invaded the country in order to extend its control. The U.S. was alarmed by this and reacted by supporting one of the Chinese armies fighting against the invaders. The U.S. also restricted its trade with Japan.

By 1941, Japan was suffering from a shortage of essential materials. It wanted to expand its territory by taking advantage of the war in Europe that had broken out two years earlier. Indo-China was a French colony in Southeast Asia. However, the French had been defeated by Nazi Germany and could not prevent Japan from taking control of this territory in the Pacific. This alarmed the U.S. and Britain, since the latter had its own colonies not far away in Malaya and

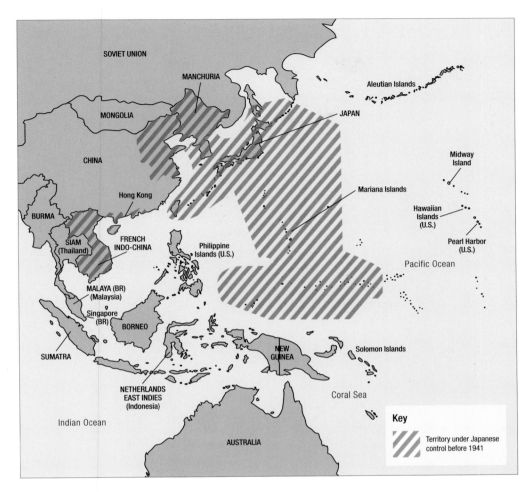

This map shows the parts of Asia that were held by Britain, France, the Netherlands, and the U.S. ("BR" for British and "U.S." for American). If Japan could take control of the natural resources that were available here, it would be in a strong position to conquer China. Admiral Isorku Yamamoto, the commander of the Japanese navy, planned a surprise attack on the U.S. at the same time.

Singapore. They reacted by freezing all Japanese funds under their control. The supply of U.S. oil to Japan was also stopped, which forced Japan into a difficult position. Japan wanted to modernize, but unlike some of the European powers, it lacked natural resources and 66 percent of its oil came from the U.S.

Japan could not survive without oil. It could either back down and withdraw from China and French Indo-China, or it could invade the colonies of European countries in Southeast Asia and take over their oil fields and other natural resources. This second course of action would certainly bring about war with the U.S. The Japanese military believed a surprise attack was the best way for it to begin such a war.

5

Attack on Pearl Harbor

To gain control of the Pacific region, Japan had to remove the threat of the United States attacking its forces. The Japanese plan was to bomb, from the air, the U.S. fleet that was stationed at Pearl Harbor on the Pacific island of Oahu in Hawaii. If the attack was successful, the U.S. would be without a naval force and therefore powerless in the Pacific region. The surprise attack was scheduled for early in December 1941. In November, six Japanese aircraft carriers set off from Japan on the 3,416-mile (5,500-km) long journey to Hawaii.

Secrecy in this mission was essential, and radio silence was maintained throughout the long voyage. This part of the operation was successful. The U.S. Pacific Fleet had no idea where the Japanese aircraft carriers were, and because of the vast distance involved, the U.S. government believed that an air attack on Pearl Harbor was unlikely. The morning of December 7 was a quiet Sunday at Pearl Harbor and no

Many U.S. ships were destroyed in the surprise attack on Pearl Harbor on December 7, 1941.

one there was aware that 183 Japanese planes had taken off from the aircraft carriers and were heading toward the island.

Ammunition for the antiaircraft guns around the harbor had not been prepared and the U.S. planes on the airfields were easy targets for the enemy. Although the approaching planes were detected by poor radar, no alarm was raised. This was because a flight of U.S. bombers was expected to arrive at Pearl Harbor from the same direction, and the U.S. military could not distinguish between the enemy planes and their own.

At around 8:00 a.m., the first planes were spotted in the air and moments later the bombs fell. After some 40 minutes, a second wave of 168 attack planes arrived over the harbor and more bombs were dropped on the ships. By the time the raiders withdrew, at 9:45 a.m., a total of 18 ships had been either sunk or badly damaged, 164 planes destroyed, and over 2,000 people killed. Despite the apparent triumph of the attack, it was not a complete success. Three U.S. aircraft carriers had escaped destruction because they were out at sea. The Japanese had also called off a third planned attack at the last minute, because they feared a counterattack. If this third attack had gone ahead, the fuel tanks and repair yards would have been destroyed. Part of the Japanese plan had been to use submarines to destroy enemy ships that had not been

SOURCE

RECOLLECTION

"A deep-red flame burst up into the sky, followed by soaring dark smoke, then white smoke to a height of what looked like 3,000 feet . . . A shock like an earthquake went right through our formation and my aircraft shuddered with the force of it."

Fuchida Mitsuo, the pilot in charge of the attack, recalls the effect of bombing the U.S.S. *Arizona*. He repeated a codeword, "Tora," into his radio microphone after the first attack. "Tora" was the Japanese codeword that meant the attack had succeeded in being a surprise, and that the harbor and ships had been bombed.

Fuchida Mitsuo, a Japanese pilot, 1941.

sunk from the air, but this proved unsuccessful. As it was, six U.S. battleships were repaired for active service and all but one of the other vessels were eventually fixed.

The U.S. military leaders had been taken by surprise, thinking that any Japanese attack would be on the Philippines. The idea of Japan attacking a target so far from the air had not been considered. Pearl Harbor had a dramatic impact on U.S. public opinion against Japan.

Japanese conquests

The attack on Pearl Harbor was only one part of Japan's plan to control the Pacific region. The other part of the plan was to take control of territories whose rich natural resources were needed by Japan.

The Japanese conquest of Malaya (Malaysia) was swift and decisive. Japanese troops landed on both sides of the Malaya-Siam (Thailand) border two hours before the attack on Pearl Harbor. British, Indian, and Australian troops stationed in northern Malaya were pushed back by the Japanese and forced to withdraw southward. Air attacks were also made by Japan from planes stationed in Indo-China, and in under three months, the Japanese had reached the southern tip of Malaya. The island of Singapore (see map on page 5), to which the Allied troops had

PAINTING

This painting shows the British signing the surrender document to the Japanese after their defeat in the Philippines in February 1942. Lieutenant-General Percival is second from the left in the foreground, opposite General Yamashita.

The painting is by an unknown Japanese artist.

withdrawn, lay across a narrow strip of water linked to the mainland by a causeway (a road or path across water).

The Japanese also set about conquering the Philippines, a group of islands under U.S. control. While British commanders were struggling to deal with the Japanese advance in Malaya, U.S. General Douglas MacArthur was in command and faced a similar ordeal in the Philippines. Some 30,000 U.S. troops and 100,000 Filipinos were expecting the Japanese attack, and it came nine hours after the bombing of Pearl Harbor. When enemy troops landed, MacArthur ordered a withdrawal to the Bataan peninsula in the Philippines, which was promptly besieged by the Japanese. MacArthur himself was forced to flee and escape to Australia.

The Bataan peninsula siege lasted through the early months of 1942. On the island of Singapore another siege was underway. Some 70,000 British, Indian, and Australian soldiers were hemmed in there by a Japanese force of half that number who had used up their last reserves of ammunition. Lieutenant-General Arthur Percival, the British officer in charge of the soldiers, was unaware of his opponent's weakened state and could not raise the morale of his own troops. Some of these troops were deserting and the discipline of the army was falling away. On February 15, Percival

SOURCE

SURRENDER DOCUMENT

"By the Grace of Heaven, Emperor of Japan, seated on the Throne occupied by the same Dynasty changeless through ages eternal, To all who these Present, Greeting! We do hereby authorize Mamoru Shigemitsu, Zyosanmi, First Class of the Imperial Order of the Rising Sun to attach his signature, by command and in behalf of Ourselves and Our Government, unto the Instrument of Surrender which is required by the Supreme Commander for the Allied Powers to be signed. In witness whereof, We have hereunto set Our signature and caused the Great Seal of the Empire to be affixed. Given at Our Palace in Tokyo, this first day of the ninth month of the twentieth year of Syowa, being the two thousand six hundred and fifth year from the Accession of the Emperor Zinmu."

A translation of part of the surrender document that the Japanese had prepared in advance for the British to sign in 1942.

was forced to surrender and agreed to meet with the Japanese force.

It was not until April 1942 that the U.S. surrendered on the Philippines. By this time Japan had also conquered the Netherlands East Indies (Indonesia) and had defeated the British in southern Burma.

The first sea battle

Japan now controlled more territory in Asia than ever before, and felt secure because much-needed supplies of oil, rubber, and tin were now in its grasp. However, Japan saw that its position could be made even stronger if links to Australia, an ally of Britain and the U.S., could be cut. By invading New Guinea and capturing Port Moresby, its capital, Japan believed it could achieve this. The U.S. knew through radio

intercepts that their enemy would be in the Coral Sea and they assembled a force of aircraft carriers to meet the Japanese. What followed was the world's first major battle between aircraft carriers, and the first battle in which the opposing ships never caught sight of one another.

A large Japanese invasion force aimed to land at Port Moresby while a smaller one was sent to Tulagi in

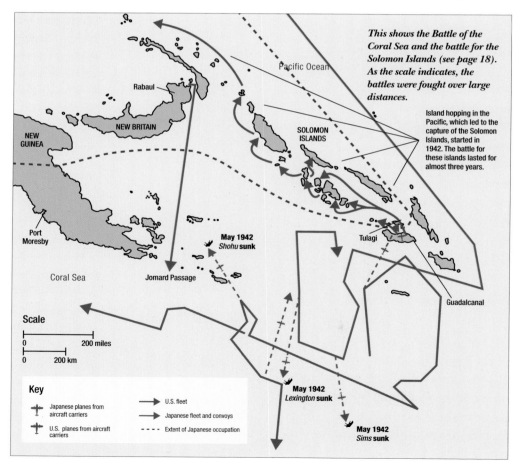

This shows the Battle of the Coral Sea and the battle for the Solomon Islands (see page 18). As the scale indicates, the battles were fought over large distances.

Island hopping in the Pacific, which led to the capture of the Solomon Islands, started in 1942. The battle for these islands lasted for almost three years.

Pacific Ocean

Rabaul

NEW BRITAIN

NEW GUINEA

SOLOMON ISLANDS

Port Moresby

May 1942
Shohu sunk

Tulagi

Coral Sea

Jomard Passage

Guadalcanal

Scale

| 0 | 200 miles |
| 0 | 200 km |

May 1942
Lexington sunk

May 1942
Sims sunk

Key

- Japanese planes from aircraft carriers
- U.S. planes from aircraft carriers
- U.S. fleet
- Japanese fleet and convoys
- - - - Extent of Japanese occupation

the Solomon Islands.

A third Japanese force was led by two aircraft carriers, the *Shokaku* and *Zuikaku*, and included battleships, cruisers, and the *Shoho*, a light aircraft carrier. The task of this third force was to protect the invasion convoys. On May 3, 1942, the Japanese invasion of Tulagi was successful, but the next day aircraft from the *Yorktown*, a U.S. carrier, attacked the Japanese force and sank some ships. The U.S. then set sail for the Jomard Passage to intercept the larger invasion force. On May 7, the *Shoho* was attacked and sunk and the next day, the two opposing carrier forces located each other and launched attacks. The *Shokaku* was badly damaged, but Japanese planes sank the U.S.S. *Lexington* and damaged the *Yorktown*. Historians agree that the Japanese should have pressed onward with their attacks for outright victory but instead they withdrew.

In the Battle of the Coral Sea, distances were so great that the commanders on both sides often did not know where their enemy was and relied on search aircraft to look for ships. Both American and Japanese pilots made errors in identifying the ships, and sometimes bomber planes were dispatched to attack the wrong targets. Luck played a part: the *Shoho*, for example, was discovered accidently by a bomber plane from the *Lexington*, which was on its way to attack an incorrectly identified target.

... we here highly resolve that these dead shall not have died in vain ...

REMEMBER DEC. 7th!

SOURCE

POSTER

This U.S. recruitment poster in 1942 shows the tattered "Stars and Stripes" of the flag and calls on the U.S. people to remember the date of the attack on Pearl Harbor.

National Archives, Washington, D.C.

The final result of this battle was inconclusive, but the U.S. succeeded in preventing the capture of Port Moresby, the capital of New Guinea, and Japanese expansion in the Pacific was halted. The Japanese had also lost ships that would have played a vital role in the sea battles that followed.

Cracking the code

The Battle of the Coral Sea was a setback for the Japanese. Nevertheless, they believed they could recover from it and go on to destroy U.S. naval power. The attack on Pearl Harbor had half completed this task and the architect of this attack, Commander in Chief Isoroku Yamamoto, concentrated on attempting to destroy the rest of U.S. naval power. Midway Island, in the middle of the Pacific Ocean (see map on page 5), was the most westerly outpost under U.S. control, and Yamamoto knew that the U.S. would be anxious to prevent it falling into enemy hands. The Japanese planned to make it appear as though Midway Island was being attacked. Then, when the U.S. fleet had been lured into the area, the Japanese would launch an out-and-out attack from Japanese aircraft carriers lying in wait. Midway could then be easily captured and used as a base from which to attack Hawaii. Its conquest would force the U.S. to accept Japan's control of the Pacific.

The Japanese planned to divide the American fleet by also launching a decoy attack on the Aleutian Islands, which lay over 1,864 miles (3,000 km) north of Midway. This would divert some of the U.S. forces away from Midway and make it more certain that

the main fleet at Midway would be destroyed by the larger Japanese fleet.

The plan never succeeded because the U.S. cracked the radio code that the Japanese were using. As a result, the commander of the U.S. fleet,

RECOLLECTION

"At that instant a lookout screamed: 'Hell-Divers!' I looked up to see three black enemy planes plummeting toward our ship. Some of our machine guns managed to fire a few frantic bursts at them, but it was too late. The plump silhouettes of the American Dauntless dive-bombers quickly grew larger, and then a number of black objects suddenly floated eerily from their wings. Bombs! Down they came straight toward me. I fell intuitively to the deck."

Mitsuo Fuchida, serving on the aircraft carrier *Akagi*, watched the Battle of Midway from June 4 to 7, 1942.

Admiral Nimitz, knew that an attack was being planned. However, he was not certain that Midway was the target. So as a test, U.S. forces on Midway were ordered to send a radio message saying their freshwater supply equipment had

These are the smouldering remains of the Japanese cruiser, **Mikuma,** *which was destroyed in the Battle of Midway.*

broken down. When Japanese messages, ordering extra supplies of water, were decoded, Nimitz knew that his guess was correct. He sent the U.S. fleet to Midway and the Japanese suffered from the surprise attack, losing four carriers, over 300 aircraft, a cruiser, and 3,500 men. The U.S. lost one carrier, one destroyer, nearly 150 planes, and 362 men. The Battle of Midway, the first defeat of Japan by the U.S., was a turning point in the Pacific War. The U.S.'s success at Midway depended on cracking Japan's naval

code. After Pearl Harbor, this task had become crucial. It took months to achieve. The first success, decoding messages indicating the Japanese intention to capture Port Moresby, led to the Battle of the Coral Sea. The Japanese changed their code after the Battle of Midway, and it was not until 1943 that the U.S. broke the new naval code. The Japanese army code took until early 1944 to crack.

Guadalcanal

The Battle of Midway took place in early June 1942. Within two months another important battle had begun, this time on land and at sea, for control of one of the small Solomon Islands (see the map on page 21). The island was Guadalcanal and the U.S. had learned that the Japanese were building an airstrip there. If the airstrip was completed, the Japanese could fly from it to attack the Allied forces that were using Australia as their base in the southern Pacific. If the Allies could hold Guadalcanal, it would be their first victory against Japan on land. Together with the success at Midway, it would strengthen their belief that Japan could be defeated. In this way, and as would be the case with other small Pacific islands, Guadalcanal became a trial of strength and was viciously fought over by forces that were each determined to succeed.

The battle for the island was the first real test between the land forces of Japan and the U.S., but the final outcome also depended on what happened at sea. The opposing armies

*This is the Japanese cargo ship **Kinugawa Maru**, which was sunk at Guadalcanal.*

that landed on Guadalcanal could not survive without supplies of food and equipment. Japanese supplies came in on convoys of ships from Rabaul (see map on page 10), nicknamed the "Tokyo Express" by the Allies. The U.S. had captured an airfield on the island

On Guadalcanal, Japanese forces came within 984 yards (900 meters) of the airfield but failed to recapture it, and their own supply problems finally forced them to withdraw from the island. Around 10,000 Japanese troops died fighting and the U.S. lost 1,600

Allied soldiers disembark; the battle began after they captured the half-completed Japanese airfield.

and used this to receive supplies from aircraft carriers. There were seven naval battles for control of the sea, and although neither side gained a decisive victory, the U.S. managed to increase the size of their forces on the island and keep them supplied.

men and inflicted a defeat from which the Japanese never recovered. During the battle for Guadalcanal, the provision of supplies was vital for both sides and affected the final outcome. More generally, the ability of the U.S. to secure supplies and equipment played a large part in its overall victory in the Pacific War.

Victims of war

Civilians have often been the victims of warfare, but never before or since on the scale that they were in WWII. The early victories of the Japanese brought an immediate end to the systems of colonial rule that had governed the lives of millions of civilians in Asia (see the map on page 5). In place of the various colonies, Japan declared the creation of a *Greater East Asia Co-Prosperity Scheme*, and as a consequence, many people in the occupied countries welcomed the end of foreign rule from Europe. In Indonesia, the invading Japanese were treated as liberators, since they were to some extent in Malaya. In Burma, there were widespread desertions from the army that had been created by the British to resist the Japanese.

However, Japanese rule turned out to be very cruel and unjust. There were Chinese

MOVIE

The movie *The Bridge on the River Kwai* was based on the experiences of prisoners and civilians who were forced by the Japanese to build a new bridge in Thailand. Parts of the movie were not accurate and the stories of the main characters were fictional. The movie was based on a novel by Pierre Boulle. The real bridge was actually built on another stretch of water, close to the River Kwai. The bridge was completed in 1943 but destroyed by Allied bombers. It was rebuilt after the war, using parts of the original. This is the Spanish poster for the movie, which was released in 1957.

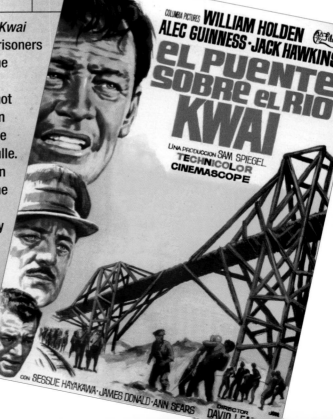

Japanese soldiers march prisoners of war with arms raised across the Bataan peninsula (see page 9) in 1942 in what became known as the "Bataan Death March."

communities in most of the occupied countries, and because Japan was at war with China, these communities were often singled out for punishment and many Chinese were executed. In the Netherlands East Indies, people were forced into slave labor and it is estimated that four million civilians died as a result of the Japanese occupation. Women, mostly from occupied Korea, were forced into brothels and became known as "comfort women."

Over a quarter of a million laborers from Burma and Malaya were used to build a railroad line into Burma from Thailand. They found themselves on a starvation diet and were made to work in such harsh conditions that 80,000 of them, almost one out of every three, died. Over 60,000 prisoners of war, mostly British and Australians imprisoned after the fall of Singapore, were also forced into working on the railroad and 15,000 of them did not survive the ordeal. Under the occupation of U.S. or the Japanese troops, the people living on the warring islands in the Pacific suffered terribly. Many thousands died as a result of bombing raids, and both sides forced Pacific islanders to work for them as slave laborers.

Fighting back

In 1943, after the success on Guadalcanal, U.S. commanders felt confident about taking the offensive and attempting to capture the Solomon Islands that were held by the Japanese (see map on page 10). In June, troops landed on New Georgia and after a month of fighting took the island's airfield. The airfield was then used to support landings on the island of Vela Lavella, and before the end of the year, U.S. soldiers had landed on Bougainville and the Green Islands (see map on page 21).

The success of these operations depended on the combined efforts of the U.S. Army, Air Force, and Navy, and the large number of Australian soldiers who also took part in the Pacific War. By October of 1943, the number of Australian infantrymen in the Pacific was almost double the number of Americans. U.S. submarines, based in Australian ports as well as in Pearl Harbor, made an important contribution through their success in sinking Japanese merchant shipping. Japan's war effort depended on regular imports of oil and raw materials, and the large number of ships being lost made it increasingly difficult to supply troops. The U.S., on the other hand, was able to apply its industrial power and factories were producing the machinery of war on a huge scale. In 1943, 22 new aircraft carriers were under construction. By early 1944, one new aircraft was being built every five minutes in the U.S.

While aircraft and aircraft carriers were being turned out on the production lines of U.S. factories, car manufacturers began to make tanks and armored vehicles, too. The war in the Pacific also created tremendous demand for landing crafts and amphibious vehicles. These were all mass-produced; the number of new tanks, for example, increased from 45,000 in 1942 to 75,000 in the following year. Other areas of the U.S. economy were also devoted to the war effort. Factories making clothes turned their attention to the manufacture of uniforms and parachutes. The food industry produced vast amounts of supplies that were shipped out to the Pacific. Output doubled in farming, steel working, and mining. Between 1942 and 1945, more industrial plants were built in the U.S. than had been built in the previous 15 years. Millions of workers in the U.S. helped the war effort by working in war-related industries. Women were employed in many of these industries and became a significant part of the workforce. However, when the men got back from the war, most women returned to being housewives.

After Bougainville, the next target for U.S. landing troops could have been Rabaul, where the Japanese had a heavily defended base; but the U.S. military bypassed this and shifted their focus northward to the central Pacific. This was because the Allied military commanders thought that, eventually, Japan itself would have to be invaded and that the best approach would be through the central Pacific. At the same time, the success in capturing the Solomon Islands was to be built upon by General MacArthur. His job was to advance on land through New Guinea and eventually recapture the Philippines (see map on page 5).

PROPAGANDA POSTER

This poster, encouraging women to find work in a war-related job, was part of a propaganda campaign in the United States aimed mainly at housewives. It was very successful, partly because many women welcomed the chance to work at jobs that had previously been considered as suitable only for men. Between 1941 and 1945, some six million women joined the U.S. workforce, an increase of over 30 percent in female employment. When the war was over, however, many of these women lost their jobs to men returning home from the war.

"I've found the job where I fit best!"

FIND YOUR WAR JOB
In Industry – Agriculture – Business

OWI Poster No. 55. Additional copies may be obtained upon request from the Division of Public Inquiries, Office of War Information, Washington, D.C.

Battling for the small islands

The first of the islands that the U.S. set about capturing in the central Pacific was Tarawa, in the Gilbert Islands, an atoll consisting of 46 coral islands. Tarawa was an important base for the Japanese, who saw it as a key post in their defense of the Pacific. The largest of the Tarawa islands, Betio, was only 2.5 miles (4 km) long, but it was defended by almost 5,000 experienced Japanese soldiers who were determined not to surrender. Their defensive positions were strongly protected and the bombardment by

U.S. forces from air and sea did not weaken them.

The first U.S. landings took place on November 20, 1943, but everything did not go according to plan. Mistakes were made coordinating the time of high tide with the landings. Instead of bringing soldiers right onto the beach, the ships became stuck on the reefs and the troops had to wade ashore in an exposed position. Japanese soldiers opened fire above the beach and half of all U.S. losses were suffered on the day of the first landings. It took three days for the U.S. troops to capture Tarawa. Only 17 Japanese were taken prisoner and over 1,000 U.S. soldiers died in the operation.

The Marshall Islands were the next target and Admiral Nimitz, in overall charge of U.S. operations in the Pacific, organized the capture of Majura and Eniwetok early in 1944. Some smaller islands, which the Japanese were protecting, were left alone but Truk, one of the Caroline Islands, was heavily bombed. To the south, General MacArthur captured Hollandia and moved closer to the Philippines. The U.S. forces decided to capture the island of Peleliu, only 7 sq miles (18 sq km) in size, in order to protect the main U.S. forces advancing on the Philippines. The attack began

SOURCE

RECOLLECTION

"...Everyone was ordered over the side. I landed in water well over my head ... bodies were floating on the surface everywhere I looked ... The sound of screaming shells passed overhead, the unmistakable crack of rifle fire zipped around my ears, the screams of the wounded ... if anyone can think up a picture of Hell, I don't think it would match up to that wade-in from the reef to the shore at Tarawa."

Bob Lilly, a U.S. soldier, recalled his experience at Tarawa in 1943.

on September 15, 1944, but resistance from the 10,600 Japanese on the island was fierce. Success for the U.S. did not come until the end of November 1944, and even in February of the following year, some Japanese soldiers were holding out in caves on the island. Nearly 11,000 Japanese were killed and 1,000 Americans also died, but ultimately, the island's capture made little difference to the U.S. campaign to retake the Philippines.

This map shows the small islands Japan and the Allies battled over in 1944.

SOURCE

MESSAGE

"Again check all arms and equipment Do not load weapons until ordered to do so. Carry your four hand grenades in your pockets— and remember your hand grenades are Mark 2 with a three-second fuse—after releasing the safety lever get rid of the grenade. Remember to help your leaders maintain control by controlling yourself."

Message from Major Crowe to troops landing on Tarawa, November 15, 1943.

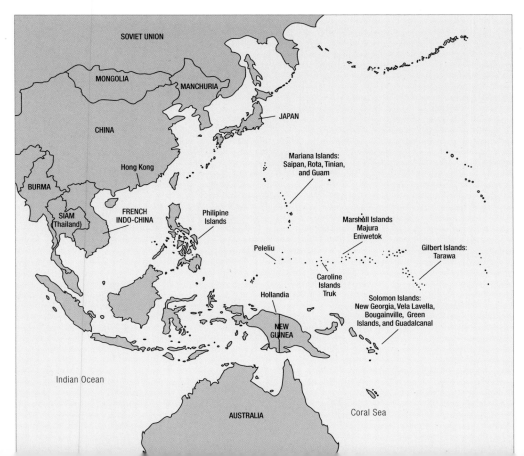

Brutality and racism

The Pacific War was fought with brutality and viciousness on both sides. The Japanese, the Americans, Australians, and Europeans all saw the conflict in racial terms and each side showed little respect for its enemies.

The Japanese were often seen by Westerners as subhuman, inferior in every respect, and were sometimes portrayed as monkeys or as vermin that needed to be destroyed. Just before the fall of Singapore, for example, a British magazine, *Punch*, had a full-page picture showing Japanese soldiers swinging from tree to tree as chimpanzees with helmets and guns. This way of picturing the enemy was also present in U.S. magazines, and in Hollywood war movies, the Japanese

U.S. soldiers train with flame-throwers in 1944. Flame-throwers were used against enemy posts on the Pacific islands.

were regularly referred to as monkeys. The idea that the Japanese were inferior helps to account for the shock with which the West received Japan's dramatic early victories. Many Westerners did not think the Japanese could successfully organize large-scale campaigns, fight as a disciplined force, and possess quality aircraft and weapons.

Similarly, the Japanese saw themselves as superior to all other nonwhites and were just as racist when it came to Asians other than themselves. The Chinese and Koreans suffered especially because of this, as did the people of Southeast Asia whose land was occupied in 1941 and 1942. Toward white people, the Japanese felt admiration and hatred and this, combined with the idea that the Japanese were a special and pure race, helps to explain the lack of respect shown toward prisoners of war.

After the capture of U.S. and Philippine forces on the Bataan peninsula (see page 17), for example, prisoners were badly beaten and deprived of water and food on their forced march to a prison camp over 62 miles (100 km) away. As a result, somewhere between 5,000 and 10,000 Chinese, 1,000 Filipinos, and over 600 Americans died.

When fighting for the small islands in the Pacific, both sides committed atrocities and it was not unusual for

PROPAGANDA POSTCARD

This U.S. postcard reveals the sense of U.S. superiority over an inferior Japanese enemy during the Pacific War. The cover of *Time* magazine in January 1942 showed the Japanese enemy as a monkey with a gun and a bayonet.

Rykoff Collection, 1942.

soldiers to be killed rather than taken prisoner. The Japanese military had a strict code of conduct; the act of surrender was considered cowardly and many soldiers committed suicide in preference to giving in. This helps explain why so few Japanese were taken as prisoners and why so many died.

Capturing Saipan

The next stage in the Pacific War was when the U.S. forces started to advance toward Japan. The Mariana Islands—Saipan, Tinian, Rota, and Guam (see the map on page 21)—became important targets to capture because they could be used as bases from which to reach and further the U.S. military's

Some Japanese soldiers surrendered at Saipan (less than 10 percent of the garrison did so).

progress toward Japan. Saipan, about 14 miles (23 km) long and 5 miles (8 km) wide, was the first to be attacked when 20,000 U.S. soldiers landed there in June 1944. The Japanese, who had 25,000 soldiers on the island, sent a large number of

ships, including nine carriers with 430 aircraft, to drive back their enemy. The resulting battle, known as the Battle of the Philippine Sea, became a decisive encounter in the Pacific War.

Aerial combat, with Japanese *Zero* airplanes against a larger number of U.S. *Hellcats* aircraft, resulted in an outright victory for the U.S. Additional damage to the Japanese force was inflicted when one of its carriers, the *Hiyo*, was sunk by war planes and another two were sunk by submarines. Japanese reinforcements could not now reach Saipan and by early July, the remaining Japanese infantry forces were hemmed in on the northern tip of the island. In one night, over 3,000 Japanese soldiers died when they advanced directly into the firepower of their enemy. A few days later, many hundreds, perhaps thousands, of Japanese civilians living on Saipan threw themselves over the island's cliffs rather than accept the prospect of U.S. occupation. Tinian and Guam were invaded toward the end of July and both were captured.

The Allies developed their own military equipment for the war in the Pacific. For example, the DUKW, nicknamed the *Duck*, was a truck that could travel through water. It was developed to deal with the challenge of landing soldiers and equipment on beaches. Over 20,000 DUKWs were built and they were used in D-Day in Europe as well as in the Pacific War. The first one was built in 38 days and given the code letters D (1942), U (amphibian), K (front-wheel drive), W (rear-wheel drive) by the General Motors Company. Many DUKWs were used in the landings on Iwo Jima (see page 30).

RECOLLECTION

"The American soldiers had been demons on the battlefield, ready to kill me in an instant. Now, here they were, right in front of my eyes. Relaxed. Sprawled on top of Jeeps, shouting, 'Hey!' Joking with each other. I'd achieved my wish. I was going to survive the Second World War... I'd made it out."

Yamauchi Taeko was one of the Japanese soldiers who chose to surrender and he recalled the strangeness of the scene after the fighting.

U.S. troops land at Guam. Two officers plant the U.S. flag on the beach after the landing of the first raid patrol and units of the U.S. Marines.

The Battle of Leyte Gulf

After the capture of the Mariana Islands, the U.S. decided to land on the Philippines and take back the territory that the Japanese had seized early in 1942. The Japanese knew that if they lost control of the Philippines, they would no longer have secure access to their oil supplies in the Netherlands East Indies. The U.S. knew that capturing the Philippines would be an important stage in the defeat of their enemy. The result, the last throw of the dice for the Japanese, was the largest naval battle in history.

The invasion force was made up of 700 ships and some 160,000 men, and the first troops landed on the island of Leyte on October 20, 1944. The Japanese, predicting where the U.S. troops would have to land, worked out a complicated plan to destroy the

U.S. troops land on Leyte in 1944.

invasion force. The plan came very close to success because this time, unlike what happened in the Battle of Midway (see pages 12–13), the U.S. did not break the Japanese radio code and the plan remained a secret.

Over the course of the battle, which took place on October 24 and 25, both sides made mistakes. The U.S. and Japanese navies were divided into different forces and there were communication problems within each. One part of a U.S. force was successfully tricked into leaving the battle area, and a part of the Japanese force was badly damaged by air attacks. Another section of the Japanese force, engaged in the San Bernadino Strait, suddenly withdrew because the troops were running low on fuel and weren't sure what was happening elsewhere. This was a great relief to the U.S., because their victory at this stage in the Battle of Leyte Gulf was uncertain.

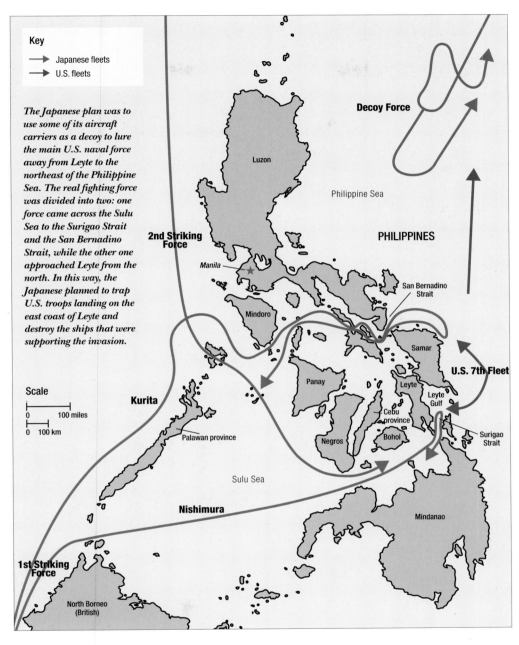

Key

→ Japanese fleets
→ U.S. fleets

The Japanese plan was to use some of its aircraft carriers as a decoy to lure the main U.S. naval force away from Leyte to the northeast of the Philippine Sea. The real fighting force was divided into two: one force came across the Sulu Sea to the Surigao Strait and the San Bernadino Strait, while the other one approached Leyte from the north. In this way, the Japanese planned to trap U.S. troops landing on the east coast of Leyte and destroy the ships that were supporting the invasion.

Decoy Force

Luzon

Philippine Sea

PHILIPPINES

2nd Striking Force

Manila

San Bernadino Strait

Mindoro

Samar

U.S. 7th Fleet

Panay

Leyte

Leyte Gulf

Scale

0 ___ 100 miles

0 ___ 100 km

Kurita

Cebu province

Surigao Strait

Palawan province

Negros

Bohol

Sulu Sea

Nishimura

Mindanao

1st Striking Force

North Borneo (British)

The Japanese navy lost four aircraft carriers, three battleships, nine cruisers, and ten destroyers, and Japan never recovered from its losses caused by the Battle of Leyte Gulf.

However, at this point, the war was far from being won and the Japanese might still have been able to defeat the invasion force on land and keep the Philippines.

A city destroyed

The struggle for control of the Philippines became a fierce battle for possession of the capital city, Manila. This was the only time in WWII that Japan and the U.S. fought each other in a city. U.S. General MacArthur, who had earlier been forced to escape from the Philippines (see pages 8–9), was especially determined to return and recapture the islands. Japanese

General Yamashita, commanding 275,000 troops, was equally determined to defend the Philippines.

Yamashita did not originally plan to fight in Manila and left only 20,000 troops there, under the Rear Admiral Iwabuchi, to delay the U.S. advance. Instead, Yamashita withdrew to the north of Luzon Island (see map, page 27) with the intention of holding out

Smoke rises above Manila as the Japanese forces set light to the city. The Allies liberated the city after a 20-day battle.

there for as long as possible. Iwabuchi, a naval officer, wanted revenge for the defeats Japan had suffered at sea and he chose to fight to the death in the city of Manila.

Manila was a city built mostly of wood and Iwabuchi planned to set fire to whole streets of buildings as a defensive measure in the fight against the U.S. The final part of his plan was to hold out in the city's business district, where there were large concrete buildings, and refuse to surrender. U.S. forces had to fight street by street and sometimes building by building. Artillery was brought in to help them and the result was an even greater destruction of the city.

Filipino civilians had no advance knowledge of the battle that would destroy their city, and around 100,000 died in the conflict. Non-Filipino civilians also suffered: in the final days of the battle in February 1945, the Japanese murdered many people of European descent. The fighting finally came to an end on March 3 when Iwabuchi committed suicide. Over 16,000 Japanese and over 1,000 Americans had died in the fighting. Although the U.S. had won control of Manila, the city had been reduced to rubble; no buildings were left standing in the capital.

Yamashita remained in the north of the island and held out for as long as he could. He wanted to keep the U.S. troops pinned down for as long as

SOURCE

SPEECH

"People of the Philippines: I have returned. By the grace of Almighty God our forces stand again on Philippine soil —soil consecrated in the blood of our two people ... Rally to me."

General MacArthur returned to the Philippines two-and-a-half years after he was forced to escape from the Bataan Peninsula. On October 20, 1944, he made this speech. After the battle, however, MacArthur ordered that no public monuments in the Philippines or in the United States should make any mention of the fighting in Manila. He knew there was little to feel proud of.

possible, knowing that this would prevent them from being used elsewhere. Finally, by August 1944, the islands were beginning to come under U.S. control. While the battle for Manila was being fought, fighting was also taking place to the west on the Bataan Peninsula (in the southwest part of Luzon), during which many soldiers died from both sides.

By June 1945, most parts of the Phillipines were under Allied control. Yamashita's remaining troops in Manila only stopped fighting when Japan surrendered in August 1945.

Iwo Jima

Weeks before the battle of Leyte Gulf in October 1944, the U.S. devised a plan to capture the island of Iwo Jima. The island, only 5 miles (8 km) long and 2.5 miles (4 km) wide, lay halfway between Tokyo, the capital of Japan,

RECOLLECTION

"The battle itself raged only a few yards from shore ... The only big problem the Japanese had at this time was choosing targets. Dead Marines were already a common sight. This did not bother me as much as a man's leg lying beside me, oozing blood into the sand. The foot had a Marine boot on it. This feeling for slaughtered human beings did not last long. It would surprise most people to know how fast the human race can degenerate to the basic primitive state."

John Keith Wells, a British soldier, recalling a scene on the beach of Iwo Jima in 1945.

and Saipan. U.S. aircraft on bombing missions against Japanese cities needed the protection of fighter planes and Iwo Jima, which had three airfields, could serve as a base for these planes.

The geography of Iwo Jima made it a difficult island to capture. An extinct volcano, Mount Suribachi, stood at its southern tip and overlooked the beaches where the U.S. troops would land. The beaches were made up of several layers of fine volcanic ash, which was very difficult for wheeled vehicles to move across. The volcano provided defensive positions for the Japanese, who could also mix the volcanic ash with cement to produce a very strong concrete to build defensive protection. General Tadamichi Kuribayashi, in charge of defending the island, used this cement to build 800 bunkers and almost 3 miles (5 km) of underground tunnels. These measures meant that, despite 72 days of U.S. bombing from the air and three days of bombardment from battleships, most of the 22,000 Japanese soldiers could get into position when the invasion began on February 19, 1945.

U.S. commanders knew that the capture of Iwo Jima would be difficult and they used their more experienced troops for the task. Admiral Raymond A. Spruance, in overall charge of the landings, was one of the most successful officers in the U.S. Navy. For months before the actual landings, Iwo Jima was bombarded from the air and

U.S. troops land on the island beaches of Iwo Jima on February 19, 1945. The soldiers crawled over the black sand of the volcanic beaches.

from the sea. On the morning of February 19, 50,000 troops in over 450 ships ate their breakfasts and prepared to land on the island.

The battle for Iwo Jima was fierce and unrelenting, and both sides showed great courage and determination. When U.S. troops took Mount Suribachi, the Japanese defenders moved to the northeast of the island where they dug in and prepared to fight to the end.

The final engagement took place in a rocky canyon that was only 700 yards (650 meters) long. Ten days of fighting took place between U.S. troops and the Japanese before the last Japanese soldier was killed there.

General Kuribayashi knew that he could not prevent Iwo Jima from being taken, but he had been successful in his intention to make it as costly as possible for the enemy.

U.S. losses were extremely high and an operation that was planned to take two weeks lasted 36 days. More than 6,000 Americans and around 18,000 Japanese died. Only 216 men from the Japanese troops surrendered and the other soldiers chose suicide. General Kuribayashi also committed suicide when he realized the island had been captured.

Okinawa

The Japanese island of Okinawa lies 340 miles (550 km) from the mainland of Japan. On April 1, 1945, U.S. forces were ready to launch an invasion of the island. The capture of Okinawa and its airfields was an essential part of the final assault on mainland Japan and a great deal of planning went into the operation. Over half a million troops and 1,213 warships were involved, and with the full might of U.S. industrial power behind the invasion, there was little chance of failure.

Okinawa is 60 miles (96 km) long and in 1945 had a population of half a million. Before the invasion, these people endured a naval and air bombardment that was the heaviest yet in the Pacific War. In one day alone, more than 27,000 shells were dropped, but most of the Japanese defenders—around 100,000 (77,000 were army soldiers and 22,000 were militia from Okinawa) were well protected in concrete-built and deeply dug positions.

The U.S. troops who first landed on the island did not suffer in the way that those on Iwo Jima had, and fewer than 30 men died. General Mitsuru

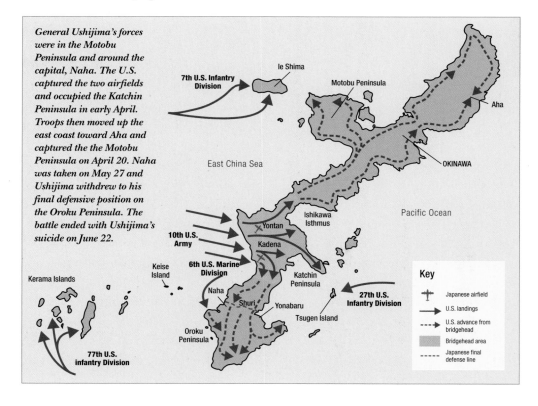

General Ushijima's forces were in the Motobu Peninsula and around the capital, Naha. The U.S. captured the two airfields and occupied the Katchin Peninsula in early April. Troops then moved up the east coast toward Aha and captured the the Motobu Peninsula on April 20. Naha was taken on May 27 and Ushijima withdrew to his final defensive position on the Oroku Peninsula. The battle ended with Ushijima's suicide on June 22.

7th U.S. Infantry Division

Ie Shima

Motobu Peninsula

Aha

East China Sea

OKINAWA

Ishikawa Isthmus

Pacific Ocean

10th U.S. Army

Yontan

Kadena

6th U.S. Marine Division

Keise Island

Kerama Islands

Katchin Peninsula

27th U.S. Infantry Division

Naha

Shuri

Yonabaru

Tsugen Island

Oroku Peninsula

77th U.S. infantry Division

Key

✠ Japanese airfield

→ U.S. landings

- - - U.S. advance from bridgehead

Bridgehead area

----- Japanese final defense line

Ushijima, in command of the Japanese forces, did not defend the beach area and the U.S. did not encounter any stiff resistance in the south of the island until April 8. It took nearly three months for the U.S. to take control of defense of Okinawa, they became an important force. Around 5,000 *kamikaze* pilots died at Okinawa, sinking 36 ships and damaging over 350. The human cost in the capture of Okinawa made U.S. military leaders

The Japanese developed more than one kind of suicide weapon, including a midget submarine designed to explode on contact with a vessel, but the **kamikaze** *pilot was the only effective one. At Okinawa, they attacked in large groups—* **kikusui** *("floating crysanthemums").*

Okinawa and the loss of life was enormous on both sides. At least 100,000 civilians, over 70,000 Japanese soldiers, and 12,000 American soldiers lost their lives.

The large loss of life was the result of the tactics of General Ushijima, who relied on pilots deliberately to crash their aircraft into enemy ships. These pilots were called *kamikaze* ("divine wind") pilots. They were first used in the battle of Leyte Gulf but in the realize that, if Japan did not surrender, the task of invading Japan would present a major challenge. Many thousands of U.S. troops would die and enormous resources would be required. It was decided by the U.S. to bomb Japan's cities before embarking on a mainland invasion.

Bombing Japan

In preparation for the invasion of Japan, the Allies decided to concentrate on the bombing of whole cities and not just particular targets, such as factories. It was hoped that the large-scale destruction caused by this kind of bombing would weaken the morale of the enemy and make the invasion of mainland Japan an easier operation.

The bombing began in the middle of June 1944 and it continued for 15 months, reaching a climax with the dropping of two atomic bombs on the cities of Hiroshima and Nagasaki. The U.S. developed a new aircraft, the B-29, that could fly over 1,500 miles to a target and return. The Boeing company built a new plant in the U.S. for the production of this plane alone.

This is an aerial picture showing the destruction of Japanese cities; the spread of fires meant that few buildings were left standing after a major attack.

A new type of bomb, the M-69, was also developed. It was filled with a slow-burning type of gasoline called napalm. When the bomb landed, a mechanism released the napalm in all directions so that fires could break out in more than one place at once. It was predicted that this kind of bomb would cause huge fires in Japanese cities where most people's homes were made of wooden timber.

In February 1945, over 200 B-29s were used for the bombing of Tokyo as a result of which an area of over 1 square mile (2 ½ sq km) was completely burned out. There were additional attacks, with bombers flying at night at low altitude. This reduced attacks by Japanese planes so significantly that the B-29s did not need to carry weapons for their defense. This meant that they could carry more bombs and cause greater destruction.

On the night of March 9, 1945, nearly 300 B-29s dropped bombs over Tokyo for a period of two hours and large areas of the city were set on fire. Five other large cities in Japan were also bombed between mid-May and mid-June. The country's infrastructure and economy were severely damaged as a result. Over 250,000 Japanese civilians died in these attacks, and some eight million were made homeless. The U.S. Air Force had almost run out of places to bomb. Most of the world, including the Japanese, knew that the U.S. could not be

defeated, but most Japanese military leaders refused to consider surrendering.

The idea of surrender was almost unthinkable to the Japanese but the effect of the bombs could not be

RECOLLECTION

"The four of us tumbled into the shelter … We lay flat on our stomachs, thinking we would be all right if the fire was gone by morning, but the fire kept pelting down on us. Minoru suddenly let out a horrible scream and leapt out of the shelter, flames shooting out of his back. Koichi stood up calling, 'Minoru!' and instantly he, too, was blown away. Only Hiroku and I remained."

Funato with her brothers and sister, Koichi, Minoru, and Hiroku, tried to escape from the fire bombs on the night of March 9, 1945. Hiroku died from her burns shortly afterward.

Funato remembers the bombings in Japan in 1945.

ignored. Over 60 large cities had been bombed with half their area reduced to rubble, and over 20 million people killed, injured, or made homeless. Some Japanese leaders began to consider the idea of surrender and the fate of their emperor if they did so.

The struggle for Burma and China

Japan and China had been at war with each other before the outbreak of WWII in 1939 and before the Pacific War started in 1941 (see pages 4 and 5). The Allies had supported the Chinese nationalists, sending arms and money through Burma. The

Chinese forces led by Mao Tse-tung (above) were successful in stopping the Japanese from gaining control of China.

importance of this support increased once the Pacific War got underway. When Japan invaded Burma in 1942, the main means of supplying the Chinese was cut off and a struggle developed for the control of Burma. The U.S. wanted the Chinese to keep

fighting the Japanese in order to reduce the amount of men and equipment that Japan could devote to the war in the Pacific. The British, who had been forced out of Burma by Japan, wanted to regain their colony, and at the same time, protect neighboring India. The Japanese could offer the promise of independence from British rule to India and Burma, and Britain was worried that this might stir up a revolt in India.

For these reasons, both the U.S. and Britain were anxious to drive the Japanese out of Burma. The U.S. and Britain developed strategies for campaigns, but Indian soldiers made up the majority of the fighting force. Soldiers from Burma and China, and troops from British colonies in east and west Africa, also fought for control of Burma.

In China itself, the forces fighting the Japanese were divided into two groups who were opposed to each other. One group was led by Chiang Kai-shek and supported by the U.S. It was the rival group, however, that proved to be more effective in combating around a million Japanese troops in the country. This group, led by the communist leader, Mao Tse-tung, eventually succeeded in preventing Japan from gaining control of China.

The war in China may not be as famous as the battles for control of the islands in the Pacific, partly because, in the end, it did not play a decisive role in Japan's defeat. Yet well over a million Chinese died fighting the Japanese, and although the number of civilians who died (many through starvation as a result of the fighting) is unknown, it is estimated to be many millions. At Imphal, in India, a crucial battle for control of Burma took place. Japanese forces attacked in March 1944 and a mostly Indian army, under British control, fought them over a period of months. Eventually, the Japanese were forced to withdraw. In China, also in 1944, Japan's last major advance took place in the south of the country. The Chinese successfully fought back, and early in 1945, the Japanese withdrew.

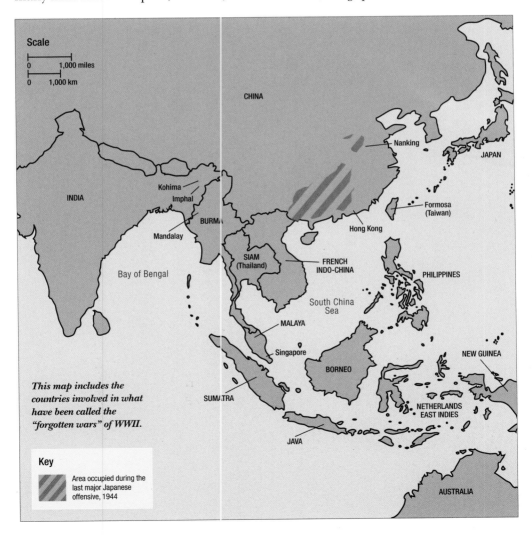

Scale

0   1,000 miles

0   1,000 km

CHINA

Nanking

JAPAN

Kohima

Imphal

INDIA

Formosa
(Taiwan)

BURMA

Hong Kong

Mandalay

SIAM
(Thailand)

FRENCH
INDO-CHINA

PHILIPPINES

Bay of Bengal

South China
Sea

MALAYA

Singapore

NEW GUINEA

BORNEO

This map includes the countries involved in what have been called the "forgotten wars" of WWII.

SUMATRA

NETHERLANDS
EAST INDIES

JAVA

Key

Area occupied during the last major Japanese offensive, 1944

AUSTRALIA

The atomic bomb

The atomic bomb, or atom bomb, was the result of a top-secret project that had been approved by President Franklin Delano Roosevelt. The project was in progress for three years before the bomb was ready for use in the middle of 1945. The scientists were working on the idea of a completely new type of weapon, more destructive than anything previously developed. They conducted their research in an isolated laboratory in a desert area near Los Alamos in New Mexico. A special base for developing the bomb was set up in Tennessee. It was such a large establishment that, when working at full capacity, it used more electricity than an average-sized American city. In total, and across different parts of the country, an estimated 600,000 people worked on the program, known as the "Manhattan Project," although very few of the workers involved actually realized the full nature of what they were doing.

The reason for first taking the idea of an atom bomb seriously was the fear

These are the control panels and operations at the "Y-12 Plant" in Tennessee. During the Manhattan Project, the operators worked in shifts, covering 24 hours a day.

that Nazi Germany might develop such a weapon and use it against the Allies. In the 1930s, Germany had been the home to a number of important scientists, who realized that enormous and explosive energy was capable of being released from atoms. The technology required to make this possible, however, was completely new and untested, and the Allies did not know if Germany was researching and developing this technology. Some of the German scientists had actually fled Nazi Germany and taken refuge in Britain and the U.S., and their knowledge was used to develop the bomb at Los Alamos.

Germany did not, in fact, succeed in making an atom bomb, and anyway, by 1945 it was clear that the defeat of Germany was going to take place without the need for a secret weapon. The Allies decided instead to use the new bomb against Japan, and at the same time, demonstrate to the Soviet Union that the U.S. possessed this powerful new weapon. The U.S. realized that the Soviet Union would be the only rival superpower after 1945. A demonstration of American power would be to the advantage of the United States.

The world's most famous scientist of this time, Albert Einstein, wrote a letter to President Roosevelt, alerting him to the research into nuclear chain reactions that was taking place and warning him of the possibility of

Germany developing an atom bomb. He warned that Germany was aware of the science involved in making the bomb. Einstein's letter triggered a process that would lead to the Manhattan Project and the dropping of atom bombs on two Japanese cities.

SOURCE

LETTER

"This new phenomenon would also lead to the construction of bombs and it is conceivable—though much less certain—that extremely powerful bombs of a new type may thus be constructed. A single bomb of this type, carried by boat and exploded in a port, might very well destroy the whole port together with some of the surrounding territory. However, such bombs might very well prove to be too heavy for transportation by air."

Letter from Albert Einstein to President Roosevelt, August 2, 1939.

Einstein came to regret writing this letter because of the devastation the bombs were to cause. Others involved in the project also came to regret their role in developing the weapon. In the end, though, the decision to use the atom bomb was made not by scientists, but by politicians.

Hiroshima and Nagasaki

Once the decision to use the atomic bomb had been made, it was necessary to choose a target. In order to measure the effect of the new weapon and see how powerful it was, a Japanese city was needed that had not previously been wrecked by aerial bombing. This did not leave many cities. Hiroshima, with a population of 350,000, was chosen.

The first atomic bomb was dropped by parachute over Hiroshima and it exploded 2,000 ft (600 m) above the ground. It was transported by ship to the island of Tinian at the end of July 1945. It was given the name "Little Boy" and it was 28 in. (71 cm) in diameter and 120 in. (304 cm) long. It weighed over 9,000 lb (4,000 kg). On the morning of August 6, a B-29 bomber left Tinian with the bomb on board, escorted by two aircraft with cameras and scientific equipment.

When the bomb exploded, a brilliant flash of light accompanied the fireball that was created, followed by a loud bang. It took only a few seconds for large parts of the city to be destroyed. An estimated 140,000 people died, some immediately and many others as a result of injuries, burns, and radiation poisoning. The bomb caused a large mushroom-shaped cloud to form over Hiroshima and radioactive dust covered the city.

The rain that fell from the cloud was also radioactive.

On August 9, three days later, a second atomic bomb was dropped by another B-29 plane over the city of Nagasaki. The second bomb was nicknamed "Fat Man," being 132 in. (335 cm) long and 60 in. (152 cm) wide. It killed over 73,000 people, around half the number of people who were killed in Hiroshima. "*When you deal with a beast, you have to treat him like a beast,*" wrote President Truman about Japan after the attack. (Truman had become U.S. president in 1945 following Roosevelt's death.)

The decision to use the atomic bomb has been much discussed and argued about by historians. The scientists involved in the bomb's development have also disagreed about the way their knowledge was used. On the one hand, it is argued, many thousands of American and Japanese lives would have been lost if the U.S. had been forced to invade mainland Japan. These lives were saved, therefore, by using the bomb.

On the other hand, some historians think that the decision to use the bomb had more to do with rivalry between the U.S. and the Soviet Union than with avoiding a mainland invasion. Between them, the U.S. and the Soviet

Union had agreed that the latter, when ready to do so after the defeat of Germany, would invade China and contribute to Japan's defeat. This would give the Soviet Union an influential role in the postwar settlement for the Pacific. The U.S. did not want this to happen. By single-handedly defeating Japan, the influence of the Soviet Union in the region would be minimized. There is also disagreement between historians over whether Japan would ever have surrendered in the way it did had the atomic bombs not been used.

The atomic bomb dropped on Hiroshima completely destroyed nearly 70 percent of the city's buildings and killed thousands of people.

The war ends

Even before the two atomic bombs were dropped, Emperor Hirohito of Japan had made it known through the Japanese ambassador in the Soviet Union that Japan would have to accept defeat. However, it is still disputed whether outright surrender would have happened without the bomb.

Filipinos in Manila celebrate the end of the Pacific War.

It had become obvious within Japan that the country could not win the war. There was a fear, though, that surrender might bring about the complete end of Japan as a nation. Following Germany's defeat in WWII, the Allied leaders had met in the German city of Potsdam and agreed that Japan had to surrender "unconditionally." The "Potsdam Declaration," as it came to be known,

also stated that: "*The authority and influence of those who have deceived and misled the people of Japan into embarking on world conquest*" had to be removed. The declaration announced that Japan would be occupied by U.S. forces until this had taken place. This caused many Japanese military leaders to think that the emperor would be removed and that this would lead to the collapse of Japan's national identity.

Many historians think that Japan would have surrendered before the bombs were dropped if the United States had made it known that the Japanese emperor would not be removed from his position. The reason that the signing of the surrender agreement was delayed, it is said, was because the U.S. was determined to use the nuclear weapon.

The bombing of Hiroshima and Nagasaki came as a tremendous shock to the Japanese leaders and convinced most of them that the terms of the Potsdam Declaration had to be accepted. When it was understood that Emperor Hirohito would not be removed and that the traditional structure of Japanese society would not be destroyed, the country announced its surrender.

Some of Japan's military leaders refused to accept defeat, however, and on the night of August 14, 1945 they tried to take over the government and steal the recording that Emperor Hirohito had made announcing

surrender. Their attempt did not succeed and the radio transmission of the recording went ahead as planned. At noon on August 15, people in Japan were shocked to hear the voice of Emperor Hirohito declare that only by "*enduring the unendurable*" could the country be saved.

RECOLLECTION

"We all lamented the situation. The feeling that Japan faced extinction was very strong. The education I received was to disappear. I drove a car up to the top of the mountain in Bandung where the best astronomical observatory in Asia was located. I took my pistol with me. I really don't like to mention this. I thought Japan was done for. My life was over. I lay down on the lawn. The stars were unbelievable, overwhelming."

Kiyama Terumichi was a Japanese officer in what is now Indonesia when the army there received a telegram of Emperor Hirohito's announcement of surrender. Kiyama's initial reaction was to take his own life, but ultimately he decided against it.

U.S. and British ships entered Tokyo Bay on August 28, 1945. Japan's official surrender took place on the morning of September 2, 1945 on board the battleship U.S.S. *Missouri*. The Pacific War was finally over.

After the war

The end of the Pacific War led to important changes taking place in Asia. The defeat of Japan brought the conflict in China between Chiang Kai-shek and Mao Tse-tung (see pages 36

Japanese children with safety masks and umbrellas following the bombing of Hiroshima in October 1945.

and 37) into open civil war. Mao Tse-tung's forces were victorious and the Communist People's Republic of China was declared in 1949.

European colonial rule in Asia also came to an end. The French were not welcomed back to Vietnam and had to withdraw. The Dutch were also unable to hold on to their colonies, which were eventually redefined as the state of Indonesia. It was a similar story for the British, and in the years after the war, independence was achieved by India, Burma, Malaya, and Singapore.

After the Pacific War, and WWII as a whole, the U.S. and the Soviet Union emerged as the world's two superpowers. A state of conflict called the Cold War developed between them. Although the conflict did not lead to another world war, it was responsible for many other smaller wars. The Pacific War changed the map of Asia and had a huge human cost. The human toll included millions of Chinese, of which over 10 million were civilians, and 24,000 Indian soldiers. Three million Indian civilians died in famines caused by the war. The Japanese victims reached 2.3 million, the U.S. 80,000, the British 30,000, and Australians 17,000. The figures do not include the millions of civilians who died in villages and towns where the fighting took place.

TIMELINE

1931

| September | Invasion of Manchuria by Japan. |

1937

| August | Invasion of China by Japan. |

1940

| April–June | Germany occupies the Netherlands and France. |

1941

July	Occupation of French-controlled Indo-China.
July–August	United States freezes all Japanese assets and announces an oil embargo on Japan.
December	Japanese troops land in Malaya (Malaysia) and Siam (Thailand). Pearl Harbor is attacked from the air, and the Philippines and Singapore are bombed.
December	Japanese troops land in the Philippines. Invasion of Burma by Japan. Invasion of Netherlands East Indies (Indonesia) by Japan.

1942

January	Japanese troops land on Solomon Islands.
January	Siege of Bataan by Japanese forces in the Philippines.
February	British surrender in Singapore.
March	Japanese troops land in New Guinea.
April	Surrender of U.S. and Filipino troops on Bataan.
May	Battle of the Coral Sea.
June	Battle of Midway.

| August | U.S. troops first land on Guadalcanal. |

1943

November	Naval battle of Guadalcanal begins.
February	Japanese troops leave Guadalcanal.
June	U.S. troops land on New Georgia.
November	U.S. troops land on Tarawa.

1944

January	U.S. troops land on Marshall Islands.
June	U.S. troops land on Saipan. Battle of the Philippine Sea.
July	Japanese troops defeated at Imphal in India. U.S. troops land on Guam and Tinian.
July	Saipan captured by U.S. troops.
September	U.S. troops land on Peleliu.
October	Battle of Leyte Gulf.

1945

February	Battle for control of Manila in the Philippines.
February–March	Fighting for control of Iwo Jima.
March	First firebomb attacks on Japan.
April	U.S. troops land on Okinawa.
August	Atomic bomb dropped on Hiroshima. The Soviet Union declares war on Japan. Atomic bomb dropped on Nagasaki.
September	Official Japanese surrender.

GLOSSARY

Aircraft carriers
Large ships carrying aircraft and equipped with a flight deck which can be used by the aircraft.

Allies
Countries at war with Japan and Germany.

Amphibious
Suitable for use on both land and sea.

Atoll
A layer of sand and coral rock, just above sea level, enclosing an area of sea.

Atomic bomb
An explosive device the power of which is the result of releasing nuclear energy.

Atoms
The smallest particles of matter, atoms cannot be divided or destroyed.

Battleship
The largest type of warship.

Bayonet
A stabbing instrument usually fixed to the end of a rifle.

Bridgehead
A defended area that extends into hostile territory.

Campaign
A series of military operations with a set goal or purpose in mind.

Civilians
Ordinary people who are not part of a country's armed forces.

Cold War
The period of tension and mistrust between the United States and the Soviet Union that lasted from 1945 to 1991.

Colony
A country that is governed by people living there who represent a foreign government.

Convoy
A group of vehicles or ships traveling with an escort for protection

D-Day
The military term for when an operation is set to begin. The most famous D-Day is June 6, 1944, when the Battle of Normandy began. The Allies landed on the beaches of Normandy in order to defeat Nazi Germany.

Destroyer
A warship, equipped with torpedoes, that attacks enemy ships; destroyers also protect their own ships from attack by enemy submarines and warships.

Filipinos
People from the Philippines.

Fleet
A number of ships, armed and ready for war.

***Hellcat* plane**
A carrier-based fighter plane used by the U.S. Airforce.

Indo-China
An area of Southeast Asia, including Vietnam, which was controlled by France before the Pacific War.

***Kamikaze* pilots**
Japanese pilots trained for the suicide mission of flying an aircraft of explosives into an enemy target.

Malaya
Country in Southeast Asia, now called Malaysia, which was controlled by the British before the Pacific War.

Manchuria
A Chinese state that Japan and the U.S.S.R. claimed to have some rights over; Manchuria was invaded by the Japanese in 1931.

Morale
A measurement of confidence and hope.

Natural resources
Sources of food and energy, such as rice or oil, that belong to a region or a country.

Nazi Germany
The Nazi Party, led by Adolf Hitler, formed the government of Germany between 1933

and 1945. Nazi plans for the control of all of Europe led to the outbreak of WWII in 1939.

Netherlands
A country in western Europe, also called Holland; its people are called the Dutch.

Netherlands East Indies
Territory in Southeast Asia, now called Indonesia, controlled by the Netherlands before the Pacific War.

Peninsula
A piece of land projecting into the sea and almost surrounded by water.

Philipines
A large number of islands in the Pacific that had been a U.S. colony. The islands achieved some independence when the Japanese invaded in 1941.

Shell
A piece of ammunition fired from a gun; it is also called a cartridge.

Soviet Union
The Union of Soviet Socialist Republics, of which Russia was the leading power. The Soviet Union came to an end with its collapse in 1991.

Submarine
A boat built to operate and travel for a long time underwater.

Unconditional surrender
A complete surrender without any terms being agreed on in advance.

U.S. Marine
A U.S. soldier who serves at sea as well as in the air and on land.

Zero plane
A small, light-weight carrier-based fighter aircraft used by the Japanese airforce.

FURTHER INFORMATION

FURTHER READING

Days that shook the World: Hiroshima by Jason Hook, Raintree, 2002

Documenting World War II: Battles of World War II by Neil Tong, Rosen Young Adult, 2008

New Perspectives: Hiroshima and Nagasaki by R.G.Grant, Raintree, 1998

Singapore Diary by R.M. Horner, Spellmount, 2006

The Hutchinson Atlas of World War II Battle Plans by Stephen Badsey, Routledge, 2000

The Mammoth Book of Eyewitness World War II by Jon E. Lewis, Carroll and Graf, 2002

Web Sites
Due to the changing nature of Internet links, Rosen Publishing has developed an online list of Web Sites related to the subject of this book. This site is regularly updated. Please use this link to access this list:
http://www.rosenlinks.com/dww/wapa

PLACES TO VISIT

U.S. Air Force Museum, 1100 Spaatz Street, Wright-Patterson Air Force Base, Ohio 45433

U.S.S. Arizona, 1 Arizona Memorial Place, Honolulu, Hawaii 96818
Memorial and museum commemorating the Japanese attack on Pearl Harbor.

INDEX

Numbers in **bold** refer to illustrations.